ISBN: 9798370845994

Imprint: Independently published
Published by Civin Media Relations
www.civinmediarelations.com

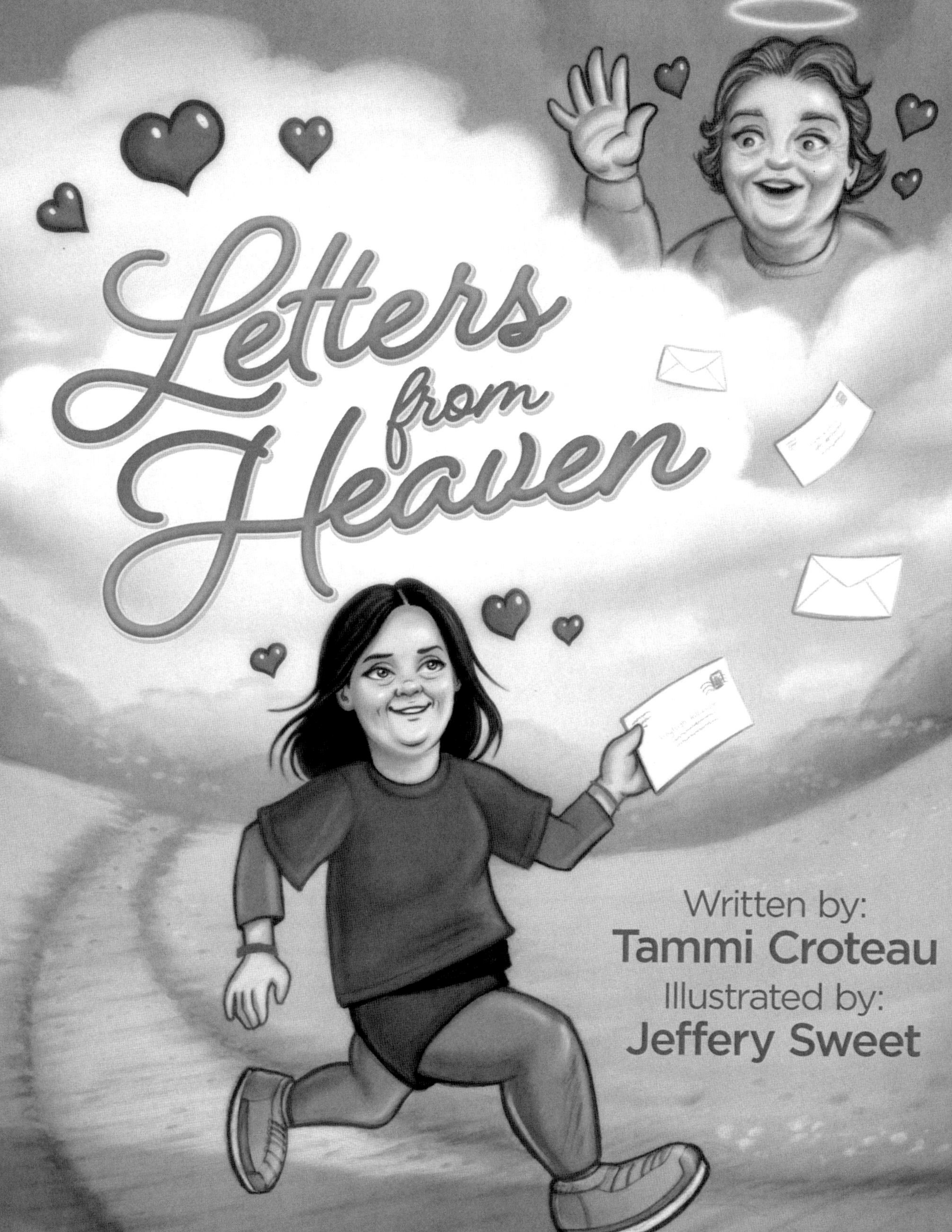

Letters from Heaven

Written by:
Tammi Croteau
Illustrated by:
Jeffery Sweet

The Kayleigh Williamson Story

My grandma is my guardian angel.

She lives in Heaven now, but she still helps me train for my races. We send each other letters all the time. She tells me to keep trying, and that she believes in me. That's what makes my legs keep running mile after mile, even when my mind says no. My grandma talks to my heart.

I always think of my grandma when I run.

My mom and I like to find races in places my grandma told us about before she went to Heaven. She had Alzheimer's, and that made her dreams feel as real as memories. She told us stories of all the places she thought she'd been. We decided to go to those places for real, and take her with us in our hearts.

CIVIN
PUBLISHING SERVICES
DOWNHOME
RANCH

I wear shark socks that remind me of my grandma's story about going to the beach.

She called the ocean "the sharks' house." She told us not to go in there so they wouldn't eat us! After I ran a half marathon in Los Angeles, California, we went to the Santa Monica Pier and looked out at the ocean. I knew my grandma was smiling at us.

DS
act
Down Syndrome Association
of Central Texas

Running is really good for me in a lot of ways.

My grandma sends me letters from Heaven to help me remember all the good things when my training gets hard and I get tired. Running helps me to stay healthy. It keeps me from snacking too much and makes me feel strong.

It gives me a chance to do nice things for people.

Sometimes I leave painted rocks along my path. I like to run the same routes so that I can see when the rocks have been found. Then I know I gave someone a smile.

Keep your Sunny
Side Up!
Ewe Rock

I never feel lonely when I'm running.

My mom runs with me a lot. My grandma tells me to push hard so I can beat her!

daymark
LIVING
DOWNHOME
RANCH

I've met so many great people because of running, like Lori and Bonnie.

They train with my mom and me every Saturday morning, even though we run really early! Lori even traveled with us and did the Detroit International Half Marathon and the Rise and Shine Half in Hattiesburg, Mississippi.

THE
KYLE PEASE
FOUNDATION
PUSHING BEYOND LIMITS

I make friends from all over the world, like Gilbert.

He's from Burundi, Africa. He was there for my very first long distance race - the Run for the Water 10 Miler. It took me almost five hours to finish! But Gilbert was there with a big smile, calling my name and waiting to give me big hugs. My mom and I have run that race every year ever since 2016 and Gilbert is always there cheering me on.

I like to finish a race in style!

My friend Ari from Fleet Feet makes sure I always have just the right shoes for my runs. He gives me hugs and dances with me, even when he's wearing an armadillo costume! My friend William always waits for me at the finish line and puts my medals around my neck. And my friend Iram always dances with me when we finish our races.

FINISH
FINISH
FINISH
daymark
10363

William and Iram ran the Austin Marathon with me and my mom.

They ran really fast at the end. When I came across the finish line, they were both waiting there! William gave me my medal, and Iram danced with me, just like always.

AUSTINmarathon
AUSTINmarathon
AUSTINmarathon
DOWNHOME
832
830

Then there's Shane.

He ran my very first half marathon with me. Now he's a coach at Mesa University in Colorado! He's getting married this year, and I'm going to be a bridesmaid in his wedding. He flew all the way from Colorado to Texas to run my first full marathon with me, too. Shane is not just my friend, he's my godfather now, too. Running makes us all family.

THE KYLE PEASE FOUNDATION
61
535

Even when I'm sad or stressed out, I know if I go for a run I'll start to feel better.

I look at those hills up ahead of me, and I listen to my grandma. She tells me no matter how hard they look, I can get over them if I try. So I give it my all, and I run as hard as I can up every hill, every time.

There have been a lot of hills and challenges in my life.

I was born with Down syndrome. Many people believed that meant I wouldn't be able to walk or talk or even know my mom. I'm glad none of that was true! Everybody is different. There are things I'm good at, and things I'm not. Sometimes people cheer me on, and sometimes I cheer for them.

But being born with “something extra” did give me some health challenges.

I’ve had 14 surgeries so far, and a whole lot of hospital and doctor visits! My mom and I have worked really hard to keep me healthy. Everybody is different. Learning which foods are best for my body has helped a lot.

DS
act
Down Syndrome Association
of Central Texas

Keeping my body strong is important for my training.

I'm not just a runner - I also swim and play softball! My grandma's letters remind me to drink plenty of water and get in my miles on the treadmill. Big goals like mine take big work!

CIVIN
PUBLISHING SERVICES

I’m not afraid to try new things anymore.

I set a goal with my mom to learn something new every year. That’s how I found some of my favorite hobbies. I love photography and all kinds of art. I can sew my own Halloween costumes and dog clothes. And of course I hand paint all of those rocks that I leave along my run routes.

Ewe Rock

Learning new things isn't easy.

It took a long time for me to be able to run a whole 5k, and even longer to be able to run a whole marathon! But I did it! Once I decided I wanted to be a runner, I never let anything stop me.

FULL MARATHON
ANYTHING IS POSSIBLE!!!
HALF MARATHON
KEEP GOING!!
10K
GREAT JOB!!!
KEEP IT UP!!!
NO PAIN NO GAIN
AMAZING
RUN
YOU ARE AN INSPIRATION
GO! GO! GO!
5K
WOW!!!

Let me tell you something. You can do it.

You can reach your goals. All you have to do is not quit. I've come a long way since I first started running. I'm proud of what I've accomplished, but I'm not done yet. I'm going to keep challenging myself so maybe I can show other people like me that they can conquer their own hills, too. I'm going to dance across the finish line of the Boston Marathon with my mom. My grandma will be watching, and I'll send a letter to her in Heaven to thank her for believing in me.

daymark
LIVING
BOSTON MA THON
FIN SH

A lot of people said I'd never be able to walk or run or dance, just because I was born with Down syndrome.

But a few people always believed I could do anything. And their love made me believe that, too.

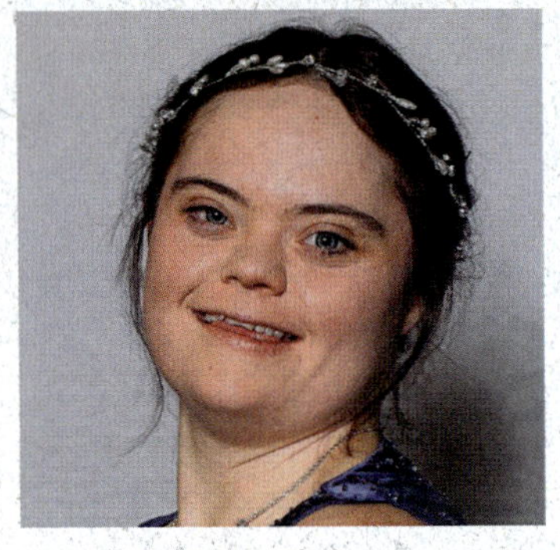

Kayleigh Williamson Kayleigh Williamson was raised in Austin, Texas, and became the first individual with Down Syndrome to complete the Austin Half Marathon in 2017. Since then, she has competed in an additional 16 half marathons including the Detroit Free Press International Half Marathon, the LA Charities Half Marathon and the Hattiesburg Rise and Shine Half Marathon. In 2020, she became a published author of a children's book about her journey to her first half marathon. In 2022, she became the first individual with Down Syndrome to complete the Austin Marathon. She enjoys public speaking to bring awareness of Alzheimer's Disease within the Down Syndrome community along with living a healthy active lifestyle.

Tammi Croteau is a writer and runner with a passion for travel. Her most recent journey to Sicily for the Palermo Marathon led to countless new stories and friendships that span the globe.

Her love of running began in Afghanistan, where she completed her first of 26 half-marathons while deployed with the 741st Explosive Ordnance Disposal Battalion. Retired after 21 years of military service, Tammi still enjoys connecting with other veterans in her travels.

In addition to several dozen children's books and poetry and short story collections, Tammi also recently completed her first full-length screenplay, Sandcastles, with B.J. Rowling. Tammi is the proud fur-mom of six cats, Emma, Briscoe, Houdini, Maya, Rory, and Dusty, and a dog, Delaney.

Todd Civin is a husband, father of five and grandfather of five to date. He is a graduate of Syracuse University Newhouse School of Public Communications. Todd is the co-owner and creator of Civin Media Relations and Publishing Services and is the Social Media Director for the Kyle Pease Foundation and The Hoyt Foundation.

He is the author of the new award winning compilation book Pulling Each Other Along, One Letter at a Time with Dick and Rick Hoyt, Line Change with Matt Brown, Beyond the Finish with Brent and Kyle Pease, Destined to Run with Wes Harding, Just My Game with MLB pitcher Jason Grilli,and 121 Days with Sadie and Corbin Raymond. Line Change, Beyond the Finish and 121 Days spent substantial time on Amazon's best seller list in their respective categories including one week where Line Change and Beyond the Finish topped the list at the same time. He is also the author and creator of 60 children's books including Where There's a Wheel There's a Way, A Knight in Shining Armor, A Bike to Call Their Own, Together We Finish, A Cup of Kindness, Courage with Charlie, and now Letters From Heaven with Kayleigh Williamson and Tammi Croteau.

The creation of Civin Publishing Services is his absolute pleasure allowing all those associated with the team to provide positive exposure to those who are different or differently-abled. To be able to share the talents of like-minded individuals provides him with an indescribable sense of fulfillment and personal satisfaction.

Jeffery Sweet is married, and proud father of three. He is a graduate of Westfield State College and is currently the Art Director at Davis Advertising. Jeff has been doing Graphic Design work for over 25 years and has enjoyed drawing his entire life. He not only enjoys illustrating, but sculpting as well.

He has worked with Todd Civin on a couple other illustration jobs like Swinging Into an Accessible World and An Endless Stream of Stories Forever Leak From Fenway's Famous Trough. Jeff has also illustrated several covers for Laura Chagnon's series of poetry books.

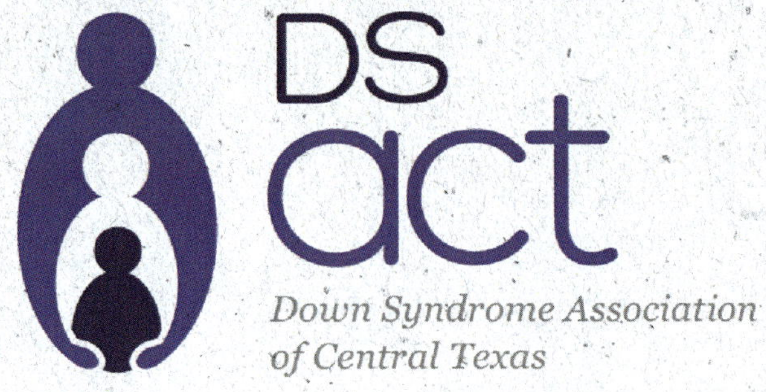

The Down Syndrome Association of Central Texas (DSACT) is proud to support our member Kayleigh Williamson as she makes her way to the Boston Marathon.

DSACT's mission is to provide education, support, and resources to individuals with Down syndrome, their families, professionals, and the community, while building public awareness and acceptance of the abilities of individuals with Down syndrome.

Our vision is a world in which all members, including those with Down syndrome, are accepted, valued for their uniqueness, respected for their contributions, and assured the opportunity and choice to create their own path to fulfillment and success.

SOCIAL & RECREATIONAL OPPORTUNITIES

We offer a variety of social and recreational opportunities that foster connections and encourage physical activity and new skills. These programs span all ages and range from kayak camp to music class to book club. Classes are offered at a low cost to members. Five social groups are organized by age, and the Comité Latino group embraces members of the Spanish-speaking Down syndrome community.

A LIFETIME OF SUPPORT

We are there for parents from the time when they receive a diagnosis of Down syndrome through their child's school years into adulthood. Our New Parent Coordinators are there for our parents when their child receives a diagnosis of Down syndrome and our Peak Speech Therapy program trains parents on fundamentals of speech therapy for their child.

EDUCATION & MEDICAL OUTREACH

We are committed to educating the community about Down syndrome. We support parents, educators, and the Central Texas medical community through our DSACT Education Podcast, annual education conference, and workshops on topics from inclusive practices to behavior management. We partner with UT Dell Medical School to improve the knowledge of new doctors regarding the Down syndrome community so that they have training on best practices in delivering a Down syndrome diagnosis and informed care for individuals with Down syndrome.

Follow DSACT on social media to see more of our members who, like Kayleigh, do amazing things in Central Texas.

www.facebook.com/dsact
www.twitter.com/dsact
www.instagram.com/dsact
www.dsact.org

Down Home Ranch (DHR) is a working ranch that has fostered community, fueled social enterprise and sparked joy in thousands of people since 1989. Settled on 410 acres, this unique community of ranch hands, craftsmen, authors and athletes all live with intellectual and developmental disabilities (IDD). Jerry and Judy Horton founded DHR following the birth of their daughter, Kelly, who was born with Down syndrome in 1984. The Hortons observed that too many people with IDD experienced isolation, boredom and lack of opportunity after they reached adulthood. These two inspiring leaders dedicated themselves to building a residential community where adults with IDD would thrive. Over the past 33 years, the Ranch has grown from a barren parcel of land to a successful Texas cattle ranch with 20 residential buildings, 13 greenhouses, barns, a swimming facility, fishing pond, archery range and more.

The DHR mission is to empower the lives of people with IDD through Social, Educational, Residential and Vocational opportunities. Through these opportunities, DHR inspires those served (i.e. Ranchers) to pursue their interests, learn new skills and build meaningful social connections. The primary focus of DHR programming is to promote self-determination, independence, personal growth and community.

Daymark Living started with a vision: to provide both an environment and a peer group to promote greater independence and a better quality of life for adults with intellectual and developmental delays. Our personal experiences with our children have taught us that even those most dependent seek independence and that independence leads to happiness. However, after high school, living arrangements for individuals with intellectual and developmental delays are few and far between.

John Poston's pursuit of a better environment for his son Michael led to the creation of Daymark Living, a groundbreaking new community dedicated to helping adults with intellectual and developmental delays (IDD) thrive in life after high school and beyond.

We're supporting our vision with a set of specific goals:

- To create a caring place to belong
- To inspire self-confidence
- To encourage personal development
- To build meaningful relationships with peers, staff, and the community at large

In four short years, we have grown from this vision to a reality. Today, almost 100 residents from all over the country call Daymark home.

About The Kyle Pease Foundation:

The Kyle Pease Foundation was founded by brothers Kyle & Brent Pease in June of 2011. Together they sought to create opportunities of inclusion for disabled persons in endurance sports.

The purpose of the Kyle Pease Foundation (KPF) is to create awareness and raise funds to promote success for persons with disabilities by providing assistance to meet their individual needs through sports.

Programs may include scholarship opportunities, purchasing of medical equipment or adaptive sports equipment for others or contributing to other organizations that provide similar assistance to disabled persons as well as participating in educational campaigns to create awareness about Cerebral Palsy and other disabilities.

KPF will provide these services directly to individuals and partner with other non-profit organizations to achieve these goals. Direct benefits will be limited to persons with disabilities who need adaptive sports equipment, mobility devices or medical care.

Made in the USA
Columbia, SC
27 January 2023